Carpet Weavers

poems by

Brenda Najimian Magarity

Finishing Line Press
Georgetown, Kentucky

Carpet Weavers

ACKNOWLEDGMENTS

The Anthology of Armenian Poets Volume II, Samvel Mkrtchyan, Sam Sun
publishers, online and book form
Armenian Poetry Project, Lola Koundakjian, online publication 2009-2020
Armenian Town, Published by the William Saroyan Society
Ararat, a Literary Quarterly, Leo Hamalian, editor
The Armenian Weekly
Encore
California English
Duo published by *Linen Press* in the U.K. in 2024

Publisher: Leah Huete de Maines
Editor: Christen Kincaid
Cover Art: G. Sahagian, artist. *Carpet Weavers*, 1998, Oil on Canvas
          19 by 23 provided by Varoujan Der Simonian, courtesy of the
          Armenian Museum of Fresno
Author Photo: Mark Magarity
Cover Design: Elizabeth Maines McCleavy

Order online: www.finishinglinepress.com
          also available on amazon.com

Author inquiries and mail orders:
Finishing Line Press
PO Box 1626
Georgetown, Kentucky 40324
USA

Contents

For my son Paul and my granddaughter Makenzie
Armenia lives on in you

Two Rivers

I study a map of our Armenian Genocide
and see what I sometimes forget.
I have two rivers in my heart.

The Euphrates flowed near Moosh,
where my mother's people cooked
lavosh, kufta, and dolma. Then minstrels
would play, and the villagers danced and
sang into the night.

In 1915, the walk of deportation began.
I still hear the screams of my ancestors,
women and children and old men locked
in their Christian church and burned
alive as an example to all
who would not yield.

The Tigris rustled past Dickranagerd,
the giant walled city with high gates,
where my father's people harnessed
water while scribes etched history
onto stone, and white egrets
and black swans found grace
at river's edge.

When the torture began, Dickranagerdtsi
women with babes nursing were tossed
into that river, their long, black hair
swirled into the brambles and stuck,
forming a holding pattern of netted souls,
faces turned upward with brown
eyes glistening into the afterlife.

I study a map of our genocide
and see what I can never forget.
I am the two rivers of my heart.

Language of Flowers

Flowers, aqua and yellow,
pressed between your Russian
and our English,
flowers tidy and dry
colored portraits,
pastel shades.
A flattened bud points
to a word or phrase,
a reservoir left open.

I have forgotten why I put them
here, these book barnacles
living on the rhythm of a line
all these years,
getting lost in the translation.

Akhmatova,
I wish I could have softened
the down of your cold pillow
in Kyiv.

Distilled From the Soul of Ararat

Once again, I take a giant step
out from the line
without permission.

I am a slender shadow
with a voice that carries
a meaning others might
think but not say.

My statement sews a hush
into the fabric of order.

The audience hides their eyes
from mine or stares at me in disbelief.

In this interval
I draw upon the magic
distilled from the soul of Ararat.

I articulate my truth.

My shadow grows tall and wide
and burns with an outline of fire,

just as earth has a single moon
to eclipse its sun.

In the Time of Halley's Comet

In the Time of Halley's Comet
with Mount Palomar a heartbeat away,
you claim your view
of the universe
from a hospital bed.

Where you dream
Jupiter falls out of orbit
and moves between you and the sun

causing the moon to eclipse
as nights shadowbox
with the days.

And as you enter the deepest freeze
of sleep, the nurse, as though speaking
through a fissure in the earth,
calls your name,

generating moments when you
wonder that all this might be inscribed
on some ancient Babylonian tablet,

and moments
when, like Venus,
you would take second place
if love and beauty
could star forever.

Yet, confined to this
single
cell
waiting for a reprieve,

you long to see once again
dawn's first light
stretch her majesty
over snowcapped peaks.

With only patience for food
and courage for water
you keep the watch,

for Comet Halley,
to emerge from behind the sun,
and let the days of March
rise to their vernal equinox.

And by the shadow
of the tree in your yard
you will go home.

Chekhov's Last Set

In a room set
like a poem
in search of its own meaning
you spent your last day.

Here life is unaltered
as the Black Sea
even to me,
to your Olga.

Your spectacles rest,
marking your place
in a novel left open.
A chessboard lies
frozen in mid-game.

The table is set
for one, and the view
from the window
is of the three sisters,
who still tarry
like lost butterflies
in the cherry orchard.

Life in the theatre
kept me in Moscow
when ill health
forced you away.

My love was quickened
by your touch. I am
left to dream of my part
in a play you never wrote.

I've set the clock
on the mantel to tick
backwards.

Each time it chimes
out of tune, I look
for bits of your beard
in the cracks of the floor
and ask,

"Was there
no one
to serve you
a last bowl
of borscht
in Ukraine?"

Season of Zebra

Whiskers of Persian cat
wake me. Early morning
trapped at my window,
sky, a cotton swab of blue.

Crow careening out of mist
caws a death message.

Dew settles like tea
leaves in a cup, lawn tuned
for beasts that travel on powerful
haunches. Violets on the shady side
of the yard sound an alarm.

I hum an Armenian hymn taught
to me at the foot of my great
grandmother's grave.

Fall has devoured summer overnight.
Leaves from the oak tree
paint themselves
into a corner.
A drum roll echoes from a nearby school.

I roar like a lion in season of zebra.
Ready for come what may.

Anahit, Mother of Armenia

Oh, black-haired goddess who braved
my difficult hours to send me a song.
Each day, you bask in the sunshine
of my praise, and like seashells
nesting on an ocean bank,
you wait for me to cast my net
and gather your choral wave of heroic hymn.

I found you on the low
end of the city in the open hands
of the ragged man asking for work,
"Anything'll do," he said.
You ached to reach into the deep
pockets of his coat, but could not.

I found you in the reflection
of a barroom mirror costumed in sari
you stole a magic carpet to cut an extra
hour out of the night then gave it up
when your sad eyes signaled you home.

I found you in a gallery. Too shy
to speak with the artist,
you hid in the shadow of a corner
of the room. I managed to carry
your words home in a basket
and watched as you hung them out to dry.

And once, when I thought you were lost
to me forever, I found a remnant
of you caught like a loose thread
between the lines of an old poem,

and you played a symphony in my mind.

Sunday Mornings
for Boghos, my father

I am eleven, your fourth and last child
and a girl, but it doesn't matter.

Sunday mornings belong to us.
You tousle me out of bed before sunup,
and we drive miles into the country.
You hunt while Pharaoh, the black lab,
and I retrieve the doves you shot.

Mornings,
where today a hunter mistakes
me for your son, and I am proud.

Then later, I carry a wounded
dove back to you, its heart
beating in my hand,
and I am perplexed
by how one as magnificent as you
could cause any creature to suffer.

I know now that I will
never make a hunter,
but I don't speak of that
to you.

Mornings,
we go mushroom hunting
in the foggy woods.
You know the trees that wait
for us with their heavy burdens,
and you pare them
from their trunks.

We take them home,
chop the succulent masses into
pieces, and cook them
in garlic, sesame seed and butter.

You tell me that when I turn sixteen,
I can get a hunting license.
You say you have a rifle just for me.

I nod agreement
while we eat the morning's find.

Sunday mornings,
with you and me and the dog
and the sun rising over our heads
like a bucket full of laughter.

Zephyr

Mother, you carry with you
the smell of mint leaves
in summer.
You are the mediator
between the grief
of darkness
and the utter calm
of daybreak.

You betray no one but yourself
when you change direction.

Gentle breeze, only you could
untie the knotted shoelaces
of childhood error.

Only we can worship
the wind
for its manifest mystery.

My Sister's Face

In your face,
I read Father's garden,
where tomatoes, peppers
and eggplant abide in harmony.

Growing up,
we watched him rake and hoe
until the earth
loosened her veil
and welcomed his hands
to guide seed and plant
into place.

Since you have been ill,
a sorrowful cloud hovers overhead.
Resigned,
the rake leans against the shed
watching the hoe long for summer's sun.

In your face
I read Father's garden.

We wait,
until he may once again
fulfill
the earth's thirst
for water.

On the Eve of the Death of Carl Moosoolian

A tardy goose honks its way back to its watershed.
Night is a hand's length and breadth away.

Love escapes somewhere in the distance.
A bullfrog croaks a somber warning, throwing

in the towel for the night between
stars laying their silvery stitchery in fallow air.

And the moon, whose patience has been stirred with
a knife, surrenders momentarily to a spider-like mask.

Pinkish webbed veins stream over that once proud face.
In this stark silence there is but one conclusion:

Only the complexion of this night's air and stagnant
sky shall survive. Though the moon, under heavy guard,

tries to whisper encouragement. The embroidery
of her dark robe patterns the itinerary of life's

journey. And this I know. Love shall turn itself
inside out, comb the earth's gravity for a place to

hide, then fade away forever. Desire casts no spell
upon that which can be trusted. Tonight,

even wicked stepmothers hold their breath
and cross their crooked fingers. The wish for

morning has a severe way of manipulating us into
compliance, all of us with some good, some evil.

Even those with too much of one or the other
will never forget the solitude of a hopeless

paradigm of stars crested in irregular sequence
at the mouth of the moon. There is no way to judge

the sun when one fears never seeing it again.
We beg for him and his potent majesty

to mediate any error of space or time that elapsed
between the dread of days gone marching through

this splendor of irrevocable harm. Love is an
endangered species soon to become legend or myth

like the unicorn, bold, brazen, horned spectacle
of virtue. Error transcends momentary fear of grace.

The water is too shallow for the goose. He dreads
the thought of leaving at dawn. How can

we blame him? He mercilessly plucks out his own
strength in the night until only his feathers remain.

The Root of the Persimmon Tree

You point to where the root
of the persimmon tree scales
across the breadth of the yard
jutting up in places, grazing the surface
of the grass-coated earth, then choked back
down by nature's demand to do what roots
do at a subterranean level.

You say, "It's been fifty years since that
tree was planted. My father was still
alive."

And you, my dearest father, at age eighty-four,
are like the root of that tree,
and somewhere beneath where your three
adult children now stand listening

the root that is you with your outstretched arm,
meets the tree, our mother, yours and ours,
for now she is both mother and wife to you.

Her trunk encases the horrors of her private holocaust.
We've all tried to chip away at her bark, striving
to reach that tragedy and remove it.

Yet her limbs reach upward
to the angels of her childhood
praising His name with her apocalyptic smile.

The persimmons are your children,
who've come back on this spring day

in the harsh twilight of your life
with a need to restore your health.

Yet, you are unafraid. Instead you heal
us again.

For you are the root, Mother is the tree,
and I am but one of the fruit, the orange messenger,
plump and ripe with time's passing of a season's sorrow.

Father, caretaker of Earth's cycles, giver of fruit,
grower of vegetables, harvester of what earth gives to air,
if you go, so goes the fruit. If you go, I must find another yard
in which to lay down the story of lost souls.

When you go, all of the fruit of the earth
shall weep.

Kings Canyon Road

Ignoring the freeway,
he takes the long road to
the Reedley cemetery,
the one that points
to the mountain of big trees,
the long road
that reaches past the river
of his heart
where he and his cousins played,
and their mothers
warned them to stay far
from the river so deep.

He takes the long road
to find his mother's stone,
and although he's eighty-two,
each time he arrives,
he's a boy of five again
just getting home
to discover

no more mother
watching him smile
while he sleeps.

He takes the long road,
and when he gets there,
he listens to the river's current
sing her song of the dead,
steady, strong.

The tears he held back
as a child fill his eyes,
and now the wind carries
them to the river.

He takes the long road to the cemetery.

He still yearns for those days.

He aches for them,
and for that river
to take him again.

From Where We Live

From where we live
in the valley,
the mountains are
as white and clear
as the peaks
of my father's homeland.

Sea gulls
Canadian geese
mallards
appear overhead in teams,
breaking into formations
and drawing symbols
in the sky.

Or so it appears
to one who looks
for messages
in earth and air.

Exit Saroyan

Why, Saroyan,
are you no longer
of this earth?

Where will your
typewriter blink out
the lights tonight?

When will your ashes
shower over Bitlis,
your ancestral homeland,
as you wanted them to?

You have taken all
the answers with you
and left the world
to argue over the rest.

That day in my bronze Toyota,
you said I drove like a Parisian
taxi driver.

You knew where to find everything
that was free, and I took you there,
as you sang Armenian
songs out the car window
with the fervor of an opera star.

Together we walked Fresno streets,
over undeveloped land
at the northwest end of our city.

You found rocks and stones
that spoke to you through the night.

At the racetrack, you placed a bet
for me on a horse named Misserlou,
and won.

In the last days of your life
you said everyone has to die,

but you still believed that
an exception might be made.

Today I drive like a Parisian taxi driver
only alone this time, and I ask:

Had not this earth
the time to make
another day
for you?

Time Is

Time is a season of pale pink roses
twisting their way up the lattice

to the window of your Intensive
Care Unit.

Time is a sunset of a season
unknown by me until now.

Even the wolves are terrified
and refuse to howl tonight.

On the drive home over the Grapevine,
 the mountain of angels

they talk, Mom, Dad and our brother
while I pretend to sleep.

Dad said you looked like his mother
on this, your last day on the planet.

While they select your pall bearers,
 I clutch a journal

containing a poem just published,
I wrote for you, sister. I thought you'd be alert

enough to read it until I saw how you were.
You wore the masque of death bravely

while I cowered. It was not until then,
that I understood I needed to cut

the life-line I'd imagined between us.
Like reversing an engine on forward full throttle,

I forced myself to let you go. In the car
someone said we were close to Bakersfield.

Time is now, for me to turn my head toward oblivion
and drink in the poison of your last night on earth.

Full Moon for February

The full moon ogles the sun,
and it's only five p.m.
It's a scene of seduction,
with this side of the earth
caught in the middle.

The air is electric
with impulses that vibrate
humans to their respective poles.
Night is falling, yet there is a subtle
hesitation of the sun, as though just
once, he'd like to know what it is,
not to burn.

And since there's yet some candor
left in the solar system so used
to itself, we do our best
to channel energies in a positive
direction. Even on an evening
like this, when the friction
of a half-dozen millennia
gets past the gate, opens the door,
enters the house. We do all
we can not to let it seep
into our hearts.

Carpet Weavers

It is 1910,
and I hear
the voices
of young women
as they weave.

One says,
"Let us sing
Sayat Nova
at midday."

"I, too, am a poet,"
Says another,
"but tell no one.
The Turks despise
Armenian poets."

They giggle with hearts
that flutter like those
of doves in spring,

believing life will go on
like this forever

working, casting the dye
into a deeper, deeper
purple that they weave
around the design
of a sunburst.

In 1915,
everything changes.

A nation's people
are lined up
and marched to sea.

Hands,
that could write rugs
in the language of color,
derived from herb and root
and the earth itself,
hands,
that would write rugs,
fall limp
at their sides.

Most die crossing the desert,
bones bleached, left
sticking out of sand
pointing, pointing
to a God they thought
they knew.

One nation jostled out
of a sweet dream
and forced
to leave their carpets
sleeping,

one nation caught
in the jaw of genocide,
his iron teeth
clamp down

And the breast of Armenia
aches to suckle the weavers,
the children
who are gone.

It is now, yet
memory makes the past
the present too.

Somewhere
one still collects
wool from the backs
of sheep,

and somewhere
one still weaves
a double-headed eagle
that dreams of Eden's garden
when it was new.

Somewhere, in a place
not unlike Mount Ararat,
the nightingale
sings of an angel
woven into an unfinished design,

an angel,
who patiently waits
for her weavers,
who call themselves
Armenians.

WITH GRATITUDE AND THANKS

Bonnie Hearn Hill
William Saroyan
Susan Vartanian Rowland
Darlene Najimian Minassian
Mark Magarity
Varoujan Der Simonian
Armenian Museum of Fresno
William Saroyan Society of Fresno, CA
William Saroyan House of Fresno, CA
Finishing Line Press

Born in Fresno, California, **Brenda Najimian Magarity** is a second-generation Armenian American, daughter of a homemaker and a drycleaner/hat-blocker. When she was in her mid-twenties she became the driver for author William Saroyan. This friendship increased her passion for writing and her interest in her Armenian heritage. A former high school English teacher, she has published poetry, essays, and stories in various online and literary journals and has participated in two documentaries about Saroyan.

www.ingramcontent.com/pod-product-compliance
Lightning Source LLC
Chambersburg PA
CBHW022051080426
42734CB00009B/1297